PRINCE HARRY BOOK

THE BIOGRAPHY OF PRINCE HARRY

DAN HUEGHAN

All Rights Reserved

No part of this publication may be reproduced, distributed, or transmitted in any form or by any means, including photocopying, recording, or other electronic or mechanical methods, without the prior written permission of the publisher, except in the case of brief quotations embodied in critical reviews and certain other noncommercial uses permitted by copyright law.

Copyright © Dan Hueghan 2022

TABLE OF CONTENTS

CHAPTER 1

CHAPTER 2

CHAPTER 3

CHAPTER 4

CHAPTER 5

CHAPTER 6

CHAPTER 7

CHAPTER 1
Early Life

Harry Charles Albert David, Duke of Sussex, often known as Prince Harry, is a member of the British royal family. He is the youngest child of King Charles III and Diana, Princess of Wales, who was Charles' first wife. He comes in at position five in the British throne's line of succession.

The Prince of Wales (later King Charles III) and his first wife, Diana, Princess of Wales, had their second child, Prince Harry, on September 15, 1984, at 4:20 pm at the Lindo Wing of St Mary's Hospital in Paddington, London.

The Archbishop of Canterbury, Robert Runcie, baptized him on December 21, 1984, at St. George's Chapel at Windsor Castle as Henry Charles Albert David. He was called

"Harry" by family, friends, and the general public as a child.

William and Harry were reared at Highgrove House in Gloucestershire and Kensington Palace in London.

In comparison to earlier royal children, Diana wanted him and his brother to have a wider variety of experiences and a deeper grasp of everyday life. She brought them to places like McDonald's, Walt Disney World, AIDS clinics, and destitute shelters.

Harry attended independent schools for his education, much like his father and brother. He began his education at the Wetherby School and Jane Mynors Nursery School in London. After that, he went to Berkshire's Ludgrove School.

His admission to Eton College followed his success on the entrance tests. Harry's grandparents, father, two uncles, and two cousins had all attended Gordonstoun until the Mountbatten-Windsors decided to send Harry there instead of their habit of doing so.

Harry did, however, continue in the family's and the Spencers' footsteps since both Diana's father and brother went to Eton. In what became known as the "pressure cooker arrangement," the royal family and the tabloid press agreed that Harry would be let to study without interference in return for sporadic picture ops. This was also the situation for his brother.

From an early age, he traveled with his parents on business trips; in 1985, they made their first trip to Italy. In 1991 and 1998, he also went to Canada with his family.

In 1996, Harry's parents were divorced. The next year, his mother perished in a vehicle accident in Paris. When their mother passed away, the Prince of Wales informed Harry and William when they were visiting him at Balmoral.

Harry, then 12 years old, walked behind the funeral cortège from Kensington Palace to Westminster Abbey with his father, brother, paternal grandpa, Prince Philip, Duke of Edinburgh, and maternal uncle, Charles Spencer, 9th Earl Spencer.

Harry graduated from Eton in June 2003 with two A-Levels, earning a B in art and a D in geography after deciding to forgo the history of art at AS level. He has been referred to be "a top-tier athlete" and has competed in rugby union and polo.

He was a "poor student," according to one of his former instructors, Sarah Forsyth, who also claimed that Eton staff members plotted to assist him to cheat on tests.

Harry and Eton both refuted the allegations. The prince "agreed the prince had received aid in preparing his A-level 'expressive' project, which he needed to pass to guarantee his place at Sandhurst," according to the tribunal, which did not rule on the cheating accusation.

While attending Eton, Harry also enlisted in the Combined Cadet Force. He was promoted to cadet officer in his last year and led the corps' yearly procession at the tattoo.

Harry took a year out from school after graduating, and while there, he worked as a jackaroo on a cattle ranch and took part in a polo match between Young England and Young Australia.

He also went to Lesotho, where he made the documentary The Forgotten Kingdom and helped orphaned kids.

CHAPTER 2

Personal Life

BACHELORHOOD

In an interview for his 21st birthday, Harry was referred to as dating Chelsy Davy, the daughter of Zimbabwean businessman Charles Davy who resides in South Africa.

Harry said he "would love to tell everyone how amazing she is but once I start talking about that, I have left myself open. There is truth and there are lies and unfortunately, I cannot get the truth across."

Harry's Operational Service Medal for Afghanistan was presented to him in front of Davy, who also saw him earn his flying wings from his father during his graduation.

Early in 2009, it was announced that the couple had broken up following a five-year romance.

Introducing him to Cressida Bonas, an actress and model who is the granddaughter of Edward Curzon, 6th Earl Howe, was Harry's cousin, Princess Eugenie, in May 2012. The pair reportedly split ways amicably on April 30, 2014.

FATHERHOOD AND MARITAL RELATIONS

In July 2016, Prince Harry and American actress Meghan Markle started dating. The prince asked his communications director to state on his behalf in November to convey his worry with negative and untrue remarks made about his girlfriend in the media and online.

At the Invictus Games in Toronto in September 2017, Prince Harry and Markle made their first public appearance together.

In a statement made on November 27, 2017, Harry's father, Prince Charles, confirmed their engagement. Having a person of mixed racial heritage as a member of the royal family has received generally favorable remarks, particularly from Commonwealth nations where a significant portion of the population is of mixed or native descent.

The wedding ceremony took place at Windsor Castle's St. George's Chapel on May 19, 2018. Three days previous to the wedding, the pair said their vows in their garden in secret in the presence of the Archbishop of Canterbury, as they subsequently admitted in the televised interview Oprah had with Meghan and Harry in 2021.

However, this prior exchange of vows was not a recognized marriage by the government or a recognized religion.

According to reports, it was pre-arranged that any extra money made from the BBC's broadcast of the wedding would be donated to the newlyweds' charity of choice. Feeding Britain, which sends food packages to families experiencing hunger, was nominated to receive £90,000 from the BBC in April 2020.

On the grounds of Kensington Palace in London, the Duke and Duchess first resided at Nottingham Cottage. Then they relocated to Frogmore Cottage in Windsor Castle's Home Park. The Sovereign Grant was used to pay for the £2.4 million refurbishment of the cottage by the Crown Estate, with further costs beyond restoration and routine maintenance eventually reimbursed by the Duke.

Archie Mountbatten-Windsor, the Duke and Duchess's son, was born on May 6, 2019. On March 31, 2020, the Sussexes stopped "undertaking formal activities on behalf of the Queen," and their office was relocated to Buckingham Palace.

After spending some time in both Canada and the US, the pair purchased a home in Montecito, California's Riven Rock neighborhood in June 2020. There, they had a chicken coop filled with chickens they rescued from industrial farms. The Duchess lost the baby the following month. Their daughter Lilibet Mountbatten-Windsor was born on June 4, 2021.

The Duke and Duchess have two Beagles called Guy and Mamma Mia, as well as a Labrador named Pula.

The daughters of Major Nicholas van Cutsem, Hugh van Cutsem's son, and Jake Warren, Harry's mother's godson, whose father is the Queen's horse racing manager, are among the "five or six" children for whom he serves as godfather.

In May 2020, he was named the godfather of Charlie van Straubenzee's first-born daughter.

WEALTH AND INHERITANCE

95% of Harry and Meghan's income at the time of their declaration that they would "step aside" as senior members of the royal family in 2020 came from the £2.3 million that Harry's father, Charles, gave them each year as part of his income from the Duchy of Cornwall.

On their respective 30th birthdays, Harry and William received the "majority" of their mother's £12.9 million estate, which had increased to £10 million apiece since her passing in 1997.

The Times stated in 2002 that Harry and his brother will also split payments of £4.9 million and £8 million, respectively, from trust funds set up by their great-grandmother, Queen Elizabeth The Queen Mother, on their respective 21st and 40th birthdays.

According to rumors, Harry would get the most of the money the Queen Mother left for the two boys since William is expected to succeed to the throne and enjoy more financial rewards. The Daily Telegraph projected Harry's worth at £30 million in 2020.

Along with many other of their mother's personal belongings, including gowns, diamond tiaras, jewels, letters, and artworks, Harry and William acquired their mother's wedding gown in 2014.

The brothers were also given the original words and music for Elton John and Bernie Taupin's song "Candle in the Wind," which John had played at Diana's burial.

HEALTH

He had a minor procedure after breaking his thumb while playing football at Eton in November 2000.

After it was discovered that Harry had been consuming marijuana and drinking at his father's Highgrove House and a nearby bar in the summer of 2001, it was claimed in 2002 that Harry had visited a drug rehabilitation facility with Charles's support and spoke with addicts there. Years after his mother's passing, Harry disclosed in 2017 that he had sought counseling with the help of his brother, saying: "Timing is everything.

And for me, my brother—bless him—was a great source of encouragement. He insisted repeatedly that what was happening was wrong, out of the ordinary, and that you should talk to someone about it ".

During his royal engagements, Harry struggled with aggression, experienced anxiety, and was "very close to a complete breakdown on numerous occasions," according to Harry. Later, he clarified that he had started boxing as a means of managing his stress and "letting out aggression."

He said that he completed four years of treatment to address his mental health difficulties as a result of encouragement from his future wife when they were dating in the mental health television documentary The Me You Can't See, which debuted in 2021.

Additionally, he said that in his late 20s, he had "panic episodes and acute anxiety," and that the overwhelming number of official trips and obligations finally "lead to burnout." He went on to say that he was prepared to use drugs and alcohol to deal with his problems, noting that he "wasn't drinking Monday to Friday, but he would certainly drink a week's worth in one day on a Friday or a Saturday night."

In her autobiography published in 2021, American journalist Katie Couric described meeting Harry. She said that when she interviewed him in Belize in 2012 for the Queen's Diamond Jubilee, he reeked of smoke and booze that "oozed from every pore" of his body.

He claimed in an episode of Armchair Expert that the ineffective parenting practices of previous generations and the "genetic pain and suffering" passed down in his family were to blame for his mental health problems, adding that his problems were caused by "the pain or suffering that perhaps my father or my parents had suffered."

Harry said he often meditated to preserve his mental health in a February 2022 live broadcast for BetterUp.

POLITICAL VIEWS

By tradition, members of the British royal family are apolitical. Harry and his wife did, however, produce a film in September 2020 urging American voters to "resist hate speech, disinformation, and online negativity" in the 2020 US presidential election. This video was seen by some as implied support for Joe Biden.

The Russian comedy team Vovan and Lexus played a practical joke on Harry by pretending to be Greta Thunberg and her father over the phone on New Year's Eve and on January 22, 2020.

During the conversations, Harry criticized Donald Trump's views on climate change and his support for the coal industry and said that his decision to leave the monarchy was "not easy."

Harry claims to be a feminist. He was cited as stating in an August 2020 interview with Gloria Steinem "Gloria, you are aware that I am a feminist as well. It means a lot to me that you are aware of it."

Harry appeared as a guest on the podcast Armchair Expert hosted by Dax Shepard and Monica Padman in May 2021. He spoke on the First Amendment and how he kind of understood it, saying, "I've got so much I want to say about the First Amendment as I sort of understand it, but it is nuts."

One could "capitalize or exploit what's not said rather than uphold what is said," he continued, adding that it was "a huge subject and one he didn't understand." Conservative Americans and Britons reacted negatively to his views, triggering public rebukes from individuals including Ted Cruz, Dan Crenshaw, Nigel Farage, Candace Owens, Jack Posobiec, and Laura Ingraham.

Harry asserted in a panel at Wired's Re:Wired Conference in November 2021 that he emailed Twitter CEO Jack Dorsey the day before the January 6 attack and "warned" of potential civil unrest, but that he had not heard back. He continued by saying that until "things change," he and Meghan will refrain from using social media.

The same month, Conservative politician and MP Johnny Mercer announced in the Commons that the Duke of Sussex supported their proposal and saw it as "morally right" and not as "a political intervention." Mercer was spearheading the effort to waive visa fees for foreign-born UK veterans and their families.

Meghan described Harry's response to the Supreme Court of the United States ruling that abortion is not a protected constitutional right as "guttural" in a June

2022 interview with Jessica Yellin for Vogue.

In his speech to the UN on Mandela Day in July 2022, Harry subsequently denounced the choice as a "rolling back of fundamental rights." Samuel Alito, an associate judge on the Supreme Court who authored the majority opinion in this case, criticized Harry and other foreigners for their remarks about "American law" in a lecture.

CHAPTER 3
Military Career

On May 8, 2005, Harry enrolled at the Royal Military Academy Sandhurst as Officer Cadet Wales and joined the Alamein Company.

Harry finished his officer training in April 2006, at which point he was commissioned as a Cornet (second lieutenant) in the Blues and Royals, a regiment of the British Army's Household Cavalry. Harry received a promotion to lieutenant on April 13, 2008, marking the day he attained two years of seniority.

It was revealed in 2006 that Harry's squad would be sent to Iraq the following year. There was a public discussion over whether he ought to work there. Harry would be kept away from the front lines if his unit was sent to battle, according to a Ministry of Defence announcement in April 2006. A spokeswoman said he was expected to "undertake the fullest range of deployments," but his role needed to be watched because "his overt presence might attract additional attention" that would put him or those he commanded in danger.

John Reid, the defense secretary, said that he ought to be permitted to participate in active combat. Harry concurred, adding, "I wouldn't have dragged my poor ass through Sandhurst and I wouldn't be where I am today if they had said 'no, you can't go front line.'"

On February 22, 2007, the Ministry of Defense and Clarence House jointly announced that Harry would be sent to Iraq with his regiment as a member of the 1st Mechanized Brigade of the 3rd Mechanized Division.

Harry had previously stated that he would resign from the army if he was told to stay in safety while his regiment went to war.

General Sir Richard Dannatt, the leader of the British army at the time, said on April 30, 2007, that Harry will serve as a troop commander with his unit in Iraq. Harry was slated to deploy in May or June 2007 to patrol the Maysan Governorate.

On May 16, however, Dannatt announced that Harry would not deploy to Iraq due to concerns that he was a high-value target (as he had already received several threats from different groups) and that his presence would put the soldiers around him in danger if an attempt were made on his life or if he were captured.

Despite declaring he would follow the ruling, Harry's displeasure with it was made public by Clarence House.

Harry was said to have come to Canada at the beginning of June 2007 to train at CFB Suffield in Medicine Hat, Alberta, with members of the Canadian Forces and British Army. It was said that this was done to be ready for a tour of duty in Afghanistan, where Canadian and British soldiers were fighting alongside Afghan forces under the control of NATO.

This was verified in February of the following year when the British Ministry of Defence made public the fact that Harry had spent the prior ten weeks working as a Forward Air Controller in Afghanistan's Helmand Province.

The material was revealed when the media, particularly the Australian magazine New Idea and the German tabloid Bild, broke the Canadian and British authorities' information embargo. He was promptly removed out of concern that the media attention would jeopardize both his security and that of his fellow troops.

Harry reportedly assisted Gurkha forces in fending off a Taliban onslaught and conducted patrols in dangerous terrain while in Afghanistan.

Harry served in a conflict zone during his tour, becoming the first member of the British royal family to do so since his uncle Prince Andrew, who piloted helicopters during the Falklands War. At the Combermere Barracks in May 2008, Harry received an Operational Service Medal for Afghanistan from his aunt, Princess Anne.

ARMY AIR CORPS AND SECOND DEPLOYMENT TO AFGHANISTAN

Harry will train to pilot military helicopters, just like his brother, father, and uncle, it was stated in October 2008. Harry joined his brother in the RAF Shawbury Defense Helicopter Flying School.

He received his flying brevet (wings) from Prince Charles on May 7, 2010, at a ceremony at the Army Air Corps Base (AAC), Middle Wallop. On April 14, 2011, Harry received his Apache Flying Badge. Harry was elevated to captain on April 16, 2011, it was revealed.

Harry was made available for deployment as an Apache helicopter pilot in the ongoing operations in Afghanistan, according to a June 2011 Clarence House statement. Senior military leaders at the Ministry of Defence, most notably the Chief of the Defence Staff, had the ultimate say after consulting with Harry, the Prince of Wales, and the Queen.

He was sent to a US military installation in California in October to finish his helicopter gunship training. At navy and air force stations in California and Arizona, this latter stage featured live-fire training as well as "environmental and judgment training."

According to reports from the same month, Harry excelled in his class during in-depth training at the Naval Air Facility in El Centro, California. He spent time in San Diego while training in Southern California. In November 2011, Harry visited England once again. To finish his training to fly Apache helicopters, he traveled to Wattisham Airfield in Suffolk, in the east of England.

As part of the 100-member 662 Squadron, 3 Regiment, Army Air Corps, Harry landed in Camp Bastion in southern Afghanistan on September 7, 2012, to start a four-month combat deployment as an Apache helicopter co-pilot and gunner.

Soon after landing in Afghanistan, on September 10, it was claimed that the Taliban had threatened his life. According to a statement made by Taliban spokesperson Zabiullah Mujahid to Reuters, "We are utilizing all of our power to get rid of him, either by death or abduction."

"We have told our commanders in Helmand to do everything they can to get rid of him," he said. After a Taliban assault on Camp Bastion that left two US marines dead, it was claimed on September 18 that Harry had been relocated to a secure area.

Harry may be a target, therefore "extra security preparations" were put in place, according to Defence Secretary Philip Hammond, who also noted that he would incur "the same danger as any other Apache pilot" in battle. Harry's departure from Afghanistan for a 20-week deployment was announced on January 21.

As someone who enjoys playing PlayStation and Xbox, he said that his deployment was "a thrill for me because I like to believe that with my thumbs, I'm probably fairly valuable."

The Ministry of Defense said that Harry earned certification as an Apache aircraft commander on July 8, 2013. Harry equated playing video games to using the Apache's weapons systems in Afghanistan.

While operating his Apache chopper, he also spoke of murdering militants, adding that "we shoot when we have to, take a life to save a life, but we're more of a deterrence than anything else."

HQ LONDON DISTRICT AND INVICTUS GAMES

The Ministry of Defence reported on January 17, 2014, that Harry had finished his attachment with the 3 Regiment Army Air Corps and will begin working as a staff officer in the HQ London District as SO3 (Defence Engagement). His duties would include assisting with the planning of key projects and events honoring the Army in London. He was situated in the heart of London, at Horse Guards.

Harry introduced the Invictus Games, a sports competition in the form of the Paralympics for wounded military members, on March 6. It took place from September 10–14, 2014.

On April 29, 2014, Harry met potential competitors from Great Britain for the Invictus Games at Tedworth House in Wiltshire to begin the selection process. As the president of the Games, Harry participated in a ticket sale launch for the Invictus Games on May 15, 2014, at the BT Tower. From there, he tweeted on the Invictus Games' official Twitter account.

He and two other Invictus Games candidates were interviewed by Chris Evans of BBC Radio 2 to promote the Games.

Making sure we pull this off is practically my full-time job right now, he said of the Invictus Games. The program debuted on July 31, 2014.

Following his visit to the Warrior Games, Harry made a commitment to establish the Invictus Games, which he detailed in a subsequent essay published in The Sunday Times. His experiences in Afghanistan motivated him to aid wounded service members.

In August 2014, Harry and his representatives were there for the Potters Field Park unveiling of the British Armed Forces Team for the Invictus Games. From September 8 to September 14, 2014, he attended all Invictus Games-related activities in his capacity as president.

For the MOD's Defense Recovery Capability project, it was stated in January 2015 that Harry will take on a new duty of aiding injured service members by collaborating with members of the London District's Recovery Unit to make sure that wounded soldiers had proper recovery plans.

Weeks later, the palace announced that Help for Heroes and the Royal British Legion had partnered to create the program. Late in January 2015, Harry paid a visit to Fisher House UK at the Queen Elizabeth Hospital Birmingham and The Battle Back Centre, a facility established by the Royal British Legion.

The Center was established via a collaboration between Help for Heroes, the Fisher House Foundation, and the Queen Elizabeth Hospital Birmingham (QEHB) Charity. One of the sponsors of the Invictus Games is the Fisher House Foundation.

Harry visited Phoenix House, a rehabilitation facility administered by Help for Heroes, near Catterick Garrison, North Yorkshire, in February and March 2015.

Additionally, he went to the Chavasse VC House Personnel Recovery Center at Merville Barracks in Colchester, which is administered by Help for Heroes in collaboration with the Ministry of Defence and Royal British Legion.

SECONDMENT TO THE AUSTRALIAN DEFENSE FORCE

Harry will be leaving the military in June, Kensington Palace revealed on March 17. He was assigned to the Australian Defense Force before that and would spend four weeks in April and May in army camps in Darwin, Perth, and Sydney (ADF).

He would return to work in a volunteer position with the Ministry of Defence after leaving the Army, while he was still deciding what to do with his life. He would assist

Case Officers in the Ministry's Recovery Capability Programme.

In the London District, he would collaborate with individuals who provide and are provided with medical and mental care.

At the Royal Military College, Duntroon in Canberra, Australia, on April 6, 2015, Harry reported for service to Air Chief Marshal Mark Binskin, the country's defense chief. Later that day, Harry took a flight to Darwin to start his month-long secondment to the ADF's 1st Brigade.

Detachments from an aircraft battalion and NORFORCE were also present during his visit. While in Perth, he participated in the SASR selection course, which included a fitness test and a physical training session with SASR selection candidates.

He trained with the Special Air Service Regiment (SASR). He also participated in live-fire shooting drills with various Special Forces weapons at several ranges in Perth with SASR personnel.

Harry finished an insertion training exercise in an inflatable boat with a rigid hull. He trained for urban operations with the 2nd Commando Regiment in Sydney. Training exercises included rappelling from a building and remotely detonating an Improvised Explosive Device (IED).

Additionally, he took part in counterterrorism training in Sydney Harbour with Royal Australian Navy clearance divers while flying above Sydney as the co-pilot of an Army Black Hawk helicopter.

Harry's ADF attachment came to an end on May 8 and he resigned from his short service commission on June 19.

POST-MILITARY SERVICE

Harry referred to his ten years in the army (2005–2015) as "the best period in my life" in 2021. He has maintained a tight connection to the military ever since he left the service via the Invictus Games, honorary military postings, and other public activities.

He succeeded his grandfather Prince Philip as Captain General of the Royal Marines on December 19, 2017.

He received a promotion in May 2018 to the substantive levels of Squadron Leader in the Royal Air Force, Major in the British Army, and Lieutenant Commander in the Royal Navy.

An agreement has been made for Harry to "draw aside from Royal obligations, including formal military postings," according to a statement released by Buckingham Palace on January 18, 2020.

The Duke will resign from his post as Captain General of the Royal Marines and return all other honorary military titles, the Palace said in February 2021.

CHAPTER 4
Public Life

Harry started his responsibilities as a Counsellor of State when he turned 21. The Queen gave Harry and William their own royal household on January 6, 2009. Previously, Clarence House in the heart of London, where their father's office was located, had been in charge of William and Harry's affairs.

The new family announced in a press release that they had opened their own office at neighboring St James's Palace to handle their public, military, and charity endeavors.

In March 2012, Harry served as the tour director for an official trip to Belize in honor of the Queen's Diamond Jubilee. He went on to the Bahamas and Jamaica, where Portia Simpson-Miller, the prime minister, was debating starting the process to make Jamaica a republic.

Later, he traveled to Brazil to take part in the GREAT Campaign. Harry participated in the music video for the song "Sing," which was released in May 2012 to honor the Diamond Jubilee, and played the tambourine.

He paid an official visit to the US from May 9 to May 15, 2013. His charities received publicity, British interests were helped, and the trip encouraged the rehabilitation of wounded US and UK soldiers.

It includes appearances in Colorado, Connecticut, New York, New Jersey, and Washington, DC. In New Jersey, he ran upon Sandy's survivors.

He made his first official trip to Australia in October 2013, when he went to Sydney Harbour to see the International Fleet

Review. He also went to the Perth headquarters of the Australian SAS.

He traveled to Italy and Estonia in May 2014. He paid respects to Estonian troops who had died by going to Freedom Square in the nation's capital, Tallinn. He also went to a NATO military exercise and a reception at the Estonian Parliament.

Harry participated in events honoring the 70th anniversary of the battles of Monte Cassino, in which Polish, Commonwealth, and British forces fought. He took over the role of Prince Philip, who normally opens the Field of Remembrance at Westminster Abbey, on November 6, 2014.

On April 6, 2015, Harry paid a visit to the Australian War Memorial in Canberra before reporting for service with the Australian Defense Force (ADF). He paid a goodbye visit to Macquarie University Hospital and the Sydney Opera House on

May 7, 2015. He traveled to Turkey with his father on April 24–25, 2015, to take part in commemorations of the Gallipoli Campaign's 100th anniversary.

He performed one day of engagements in the US on October 28, 2015. He introduced the Invictus Games Orlando 2016 at Fort Belvoir with Michelle Obama, the first lady, and Jill Biden, the second lady.

Later, he went to a board meeting for the Invictus Games and a launch-related event at the home of the British ambassador. Harry traveled to Lesotho on November 26, 2015, to witness the inauguration of the Mamohato Children's Center in his capacity as patron of Sentebale.

He paid an official visit to South Africa from November 30 to December 3, 2015. On behalf of the Queen, he traveled to Cape Town and gave the Archbishop the Order of the Companions of Honor's insignia.

At the Val de Vie Estate in Cape Town, Harry also participated in the Sentebale Royal Salute Polo Cup, which raised money for the organization. On March 19–23, 2016, he was in Nepal.

He remained in Nepal till the end of March 2016 to work on Team Rubicon UK's secondary school reconstruction project and to visit a hydropower project there.

He was chosen as Commonwealth youth ambassador in April 2018, and he served in that capacity until March 2020. Harry joined the Walk of America campaign in the same month and became its patron.

The initiative unites veterans who will travel 1,000 miles across the US in the middle of 2018. The Queen's Commonwealth Trust, which concentrates on initiatives involving kids and prisoner care, selected The Prince as its president in April.

Online QCT chat sessions were sometimes held and posted on YouTube for viewing by the general public. Up until February 2021, he served as the organization's president. Harry and his wife Meghan visited Dublin, Ireland, in July 2018, which was their first trip abroad together.

The Duke and Duchess of Sussex traveled to Sydney, Australia, in October 2018 to attend the Invictus Games. This was a stop on a tour of the Pacific that included took in stops in Australia, Fiji, Tonga, and New Zealand.

The Duke and Duchess focused on initiatives centered on "women's empowerment, girls' education, inclusiveness, and support of social entrepreneurship" during their visit to Morocco in February 2019. The Duke and Duchess established an Instagram account in 2019 as part of opening a separate office from Kensington Palace, breaking the previous record for the quickest account to achieve a million followers.

The Born Free to Shine program, run by First Lady Ana Dias Lourenço, seeks to "prevent HIV transmission from mothers to newborns" via awareness, medical testing, and treatment, and the Duke paid a visit to it during his 2019 visit to Angola.

During his tour, he also spoke with young people who were HIV-positive. The Duke announced a program by the Queen's Commonwealth Canopy to assist in maintaining "an old elephant migratory path" by ensuring their safety in the forest during his visit to the Luengue-Luiana National Park.

A Southern African tour that encompassed Malawi, Angola, South Africa, and Botswana took place in September and October 2019.

The Sussexes' first formal trip as a family was made possible by the fact that their baby son Archie traveled with them.

STEPPING BACK

The Duke and Duchess stated in January 2020 that they would divide their time equally between the United Kingdom and North America when they retired from their position as senior members of the royal family.

The Duke and Duchess were to stop serving as the Queen's representatives and become financially independent, according to a statement issued by the Palace. The pair keeps their HRH looks, but they are not allowed to wear them. The official function of the Duke and Duchess was up for review after a year, which ended in March 2021.

Harry and racing star Lewis Hamilton both attended the Silverstone Experience's grand inauguration at Silverstone Circuit in March 2020. Harry's last solo engagement as a senior royal was his visit to the museum. On March 9, 2020, he and Meghan attended the Commonwealth Day ceremony at Westminster Abbey.

This was their last public appearance together before they formally resigned on March 31, 2020. Two years later, in June 2022, they attended the Platinum Jubilee National Service of Thanksgiving and made their first public appearance in the UK. In September 2022, they traveled to the UK and Germany for a variety of charitable engagements in Manchester and Düsseldorf.

Queen Elizabeth II passed away at Balmoral Castle in Scotland on September 8, 2022, while Harry and Meghan were in London getting ready to attend a charity event.

While Harry went to Balmoral, Meghan remained in London, and the pair decided not to attend the charity event that evening.

CHAPTER 5
Civilian Career And Investment

Harry and his wife had discussions with Jeffrey Katzenberg, the creator of the now-defunct streaming service Quibi, in the summer of 2019 before announcing their decision to step back in January 2020, about a potential role in the service without gaining personal profits.

However, they ultimately decided against joining the project. The pair reportedly engaged the New York-based PR agency, Sunshine Sachs, in September 2019, and they were represented by them until 2022.

They agreed to give compensated public speeches after signing a contract with the media business Endeavor's Harry Walker Agency in June 2020. The Sussexes and Netflix inked a confidential business agreement in September 2020 "to produce scripted and unscripted shows, cinema, documentaries, and children content for the streaming giant."

The pair will present a special edition of Time 100 Talks with the topic "Engineering a Better World" in October 2020. The Duke and Duchess struck a multi-year agreement with Spotify in December 2020 to host and create their shows via their audio production firm, Archewell Audio. The pair published a Christmas special on the service in December 2020.

Harry will serve as the organization's first chief impact officer, according to San Francisco-based BetterUp, a mental health start-up that facilitates connections between clients and coaches.

Among other responsibilities, Harry "will help promote mental fitness and expand the company's roster of coaches and customers." Harry continued, citing his own experience working with a BetterUp coach as being "invaluable."

The Aspen Institute's Commission on Information Disorder nominated Harry as a commissioner the same month to lead a six-month investigation into the prevalence of misinformation and disinformation in the country.

The study's findings, which included 15 recommendations, were released in November 2021. The Great Resignation, a recent trend in which people are quitting their jobs, was something that needed to be celebrated, Harry said in an interview with Fast Company the following month while serving as BetterUp's chief impact officer.

However, his comments were criticized for coming from a position of privilege. Reports of complaints from the business's instructors in April 2022 over the new measures used for measuring their performance and the secrecy surrounding Harry's true position in the organization first surfaced.

It was revealed in April 2019 that Harry and Oprah Winfrey were co-creating and executive-producing a documentary series on mental health that was previously scheduled to premiere in 2020 on Apple TV+.

The series, named The Me You Can't See, will be published on May 21, 2021, and it was subsequently revealed. The following month, UCAS recorded a rise in the proportion of applicants disclosing mental health conditions on their university applications, attributing the development to self-help literature and Prince Harry's admissions of his battles with "panic attacks and anxiety."

Harry and Meghan traveled to New York in September 2021. While there, they met with

Amina J. Mohammed, the deputy secretary-general of the United Nations, and Linda Thomas-Greenfield, the ambassador of the United States to the United Nations.

They also visited the 9/11 Memorial with New York governor Kathy Hochul and mayor Bill de Blasio. Harry and Meghan made an official announcement in October 2021 about their collaboration with New York City-based Ethic, a sustainable investing company that also looks after the couple's portfolio.

Harry and Meghan incorporated 11 companies and a trust beginning in early 2020, including Orinoco Publishing LLC and Peca Publishing LLC to hold the rights to their books as well as Cobblestone Lane LLC and IPHW LLC to hold the foundation's logos, according to state filings from Delaware, where the couple's Archewell foundation is registered.

In July 2021, it was revealed that Harry would release a memoir through Penguin Random House.

The book's sales would benefit charities, and Harry would reportedly receive an advance of at least $20 million. J. R. Moehringer, a novelist, will pen a ghost version of it.

A four-volume publishing agreement, including a second book by Harry and a health manual by Meghan, is said to contain the memoir. The book, titled Spare, is planned for release on January 10th, 2023. A portion of the book's sales will be given to charity and it will be published in 16 other languages.

CHAPTER 6
Charity Work

Environmental and humanitarian initiatives He returned to Lesotho in 2006 to see the Mants'ase Children's Home in Mohale's Hoek, which he had previously seen in 2004. He established Sentebale: The Princes' Fund for Lesotho, a nonprofit organization to assist kids left orphaned by HIV/AIDS, together with Prince Seeiso of Lesotho.

He has lent his support to a number of organizations, including WellChild, Dolen Cymru, MapAction, and the London Marathon Charitable Trust; he resigned from both in 2019 and 2021, respectively.

In 2007, William and Harry organized the Concert for Diana in honor of their mother. Proceeds from the event benefitted Diana,

William, and Harry's charitable organizations.

Harry and his brother rode across South Africa on motorcycles for 1,000 miles over eight days in October 2008 to collect money for Sentebale, UNICEF, and the Nelson Mandela Children's Fund.

The Foundation of Prince William and Prince Harry was established in September 2009 by William and Harry to support their charity goals. In June 2019, Harry departed the charity.

Harry undertook Walking With The Wounded's 200-mile trek to the South Pole in December 2013 with twelve disabled military members from the UK, the US, and the Commonwealth after taking part in an incomplete journey to the North Pole with the organization in 2011.

On September 30 and October 20, 2015, he walked alongside the group as the Walk of Britain's patron. On July 14, 2016, Harry underwent a live HIV test on the royal family's Facebook page to promote testing. Later, on July 21, 2016, he went to the 21st International AIDS Conference in Durban, South Africa.

Harry and Rihanna took the HIV test on World AIDS Day to promote HIV testing. Harry has been collaborating with the Terrence Higgins Trust to spread knowledge about HIV and sexual health since 2016.

Gareth Thomas, an HIV+ rugby player, was interviewed by the Duke on behalf of the charity in November 2019 to commemorate National HIV Testing Week.

Harry served as a guest editor for BBC Radio 4's Today program in December 2017. He conducted interviews on topics such teenage violence, the military, mental health, the Commonwealth, conservation, and the environment with his father, the Prince of Wales, former US president Barack Obama, and others.

Harry received his formal appointment as African Parks' new president on December 27, 2017, an environmental non-profit. His last trip to Malawi with African Parks lasted three weeks, when he worked with a group of experts and volunteers to complete one of the biggest elephant translocations in history. 500 elephants were relocated from Liwonde and Majete National Parks to Nkhotakota Wildlife Reserve as part of the attempt to repopulate regions ravaged by poaching and habitat destruction.

Prior to becoming a patron of the Rhino Conservation Botswana, Harry assisted in the relocation of rhinos in the Okavango Delta. The Duke of Sussex and British musician Elton John were going to start a worldwide coalition named MenStar that would concentrate "on treating HIV infections in males," according to an announcement made by the Elton John AIDS Foundation in July 2018.

Prince Harry delivered a speech in March 2019 at WE Day UK, an annual gathering put on by We Charity to encourage young people to take action for social and environmental change on a worldwide scale. He spoke on social involvement, mental health, and climate change.

The UK's first 24-hour text messaging service for people with mental illnesses, Shout, was introduced in May 2019 by the Duke and Duchess of Sussex, Harry's brother, and Harry's sister-in-law.

In August 2019, Harry participated in a Google event and spoke in Sicily about the need of combating climate change. He added that in order to save the environment, he and Meghan want to have no more than 2 kids.

After two years of development, the Duke debuted Travalyst in September 2019 when he was in the Netherlands. In partnership with a number of businesses, including Tripadvisor, Booking.com, Ctrip, Skyscanner, and Visa Inc., the program aims to "promote sustainable practices in the travel sector" and "address climate change and environmental harm."

Later, in 2021, the organization declared a partnership with Google. Harry voiced a Public Health England announcement for the "Every Mind Matters" mental health program in October 2019, along with other members of the royal family.

Harry collaborated with Jon Bon Jovi to create a new version of the song "Unbroken" in February 2020. Members of the Invictus Choir provide supporting vocals for the new rendition. The song was published on March 27, 2020, and the Invictus Games Foundation received the revenues.

Harry unveiled a brand-new program in April 2020 called HeadFIT, a platform created to provide mental assistance to service personnel. Together, the Ministry of Defense, King's College London, and the Royal Foundation's Heads Together campaign devised the program.

During the COVID-19 epidemic in the US in April 2020, the Duke and Duchess brought meals made by Project Angel Food to Los Angeles citizens. The pair supported the Stop Hate for Profit initiative in June 2020 and urged CEOs of various corporations to become involved.

Harry and Meghan worked with Baby2Baby in August 2020 and took part in a drive-through delivery of school supplies to youngsters. He worked with American veterans from The Mission Continues Service Platoons to deliver meals in Compton, California, with Compton Veterans and the Walker Family Events Foundation during the UK's Remembrance Week in November 2020.

In April 2021, it was revealed that Harry and Meghan will serve as the campaign chairmen for Global Citizen's Vax Live: The Concert to Reunite the World, an occasion intended to expand access to COVID-19 vaccines.

They also declared their support for a fundraising for vaccination equality organized by the same group and sent an open letter to the CEOs of the pharmaceutical sector pleading with them to solve the vaccine equity challenge.

Later that month, he provided narration for "Hope Starts Here," a special movie that

African Parks re-released in honor of Earth Day.

In it, he encouraged organizations and people to protect biodiversity and paid homage to his grandpa Prince Philip for his conservationist work. In May 2021, he publicly expressed his support for Peak State, a mental fitness program that aims to provide skills and resources for managing mental wellness. He assisted in its founding.

Harry has volunteered with the HALO Trust, an organization that clears war-related debris, mainly landmines, as his mother did. With the NGO, he had previously spent two days learning about their work and mine-clearing methods in a minefield in Mozambique.

He was chosen as the charity's 25th Anniversary Appeal's patron in 2013. He held the Landmine Free 2025 event in April 2017 at Kensington Palace, when the UK government announced an increase in funding for demining initiatives.

He traveled to a demining site in Angola in September 2019, the same nation his mother had visited 22 years earlier. After 10 trust members were murdered by armed individuals at a camp for mine clearing in Afghanistan in June 2021, Harry declared the incident to be "nothing less than an act of savagery."

He co-hosted a virtual event in September 2021 with First Lady Jill Biden for the Warrior Games, which were postponed because of the COVID-19 pandemic. The following month, Harry and Meghan gave another speech at the Global Citizen Live event in favor of vaccination equality.

He opposed oil extraction in the Okavango River in an opinion piece for The Washington Post in October 2021. Harry and his wife, together with Tedros

Adhanom, the director-general of the World Health Organization, sent an open letter in the same month urging the G20 leaders to speed up preparations for the worldwide distribution of COVID-19 vaccinations in advance of the 2021 G20 summit in Rome.

Following criticism of Spotify's handling of COVID-19 disinformation, Harry and Meghan said in January 2022 that they had started "raising concerns" about the matter on the site as of April 2021.

They signed an open letter, which was released by the People's Vaccine Alliance in March 2022, advocating for free access to COVID-19 vaccinations on a worldwide scale and criticizing the UK, EU, and Switzerland for rejecting a waiver that would enable vaccine intellectual property restrictions to be repealed.

Harry started his non-profit Travalyst in April 2022, and in a video that aired on

Mori Television and included Rhys Darby and Dave Fane, he urged people to travel responsibly.

As president of African Parks, Harry traveled to Africa in August 2022 to greet a group of "U.S. officials, environmentalists, and benefactors as they visit protected wildlife and natural regions."

SPORT

Harry likes to participate in a variety of activities, such as competitive polo, skiing, and motocross. He has played in polo matches to support philanthropic organizations, like his brother and father.

Harry is a big admirer of rugby football as well. He backed England's quest to host the 2015 Rugby World Cup for rugby union, and he also gave the trophy out at the 2019 Challenge Cup finals for rugby league. Harry received training as a Rugby Football Union

Rugby Development Officer in 2004 and began coaching pupils in classrooms to encourage them to take up the sport.

He said that the hymn "Swing Low, Sweet Chariot" should no longer be performed in a rugby environment in reaction to Black Lives Matter, as did former rugby player Brian Moore. He served as the patron of both the Rugby Football Union and Rugby Football League, which governs Rugby League in England, until February 2021.

Harry debuted Coach Core in 2012 together with the Duke and Duchess of Cambridge. The program, which was established in the wake of the 2012 Olympics, offers possibilities for apprenticeship to those who want to become professional coaches.

Harry went to the Running Charity and its partner Depaul UK in January 2017 to raise awareness about how sport can assist the homeless and disadvantaged. The Duke attended the Made by Sport coalition's June 2019 inaugural event, which aimed to gather funds to promote sport in underserved areas.

In his statement, he offered his support to the organization, claiming that the organisation's work in integrating sport into the lives of those who are less fortunate would result in savings of "hundreds of millions of pounds" for the treatment of problems affecting young people.

SUSSEX ROYAL AND ARCHEWELL

The Duke and Duchess of Sussex made the decision to leave The Royal Foundation in June 2019 and launch their own charitable organization by the end of the year.

However, the pair would work together on shared causes, such the mental health initiative Heads Together, alongside Harry's brother and his wife. Sussex Royal The

Foundation of The Duke and Duchess of Sussex was the name given to Harry and Meghan's new charity when it was officially incorporated in England and Wales in July 2019.

After the pair withdrew from public life, it was announced on February 21 that "Sussex Royal" would no longer be used as a brand name for the couple. The Sussex Royal Foundation was renamed "MWX Foundation" on August 5, 2020, and it was also disbanded on that day.

The Sussex Royal organization was being examined by the Charity Commission for England and Wales in a "regulatory and compliance case" over its behavior in accordance with charity law during dissolution, according to a report from March 2021.

Representatives for the pair said that a board of trustees operated Sussex Royal and that it would be unfair to attribute any "suggestion of mismanagement" to the Duke and Duchess alone.

In a subsequent report, the commission ruled that the foundation had not engaged in illegal behavior but criticized the board of directors for devoting a "substantial proportion of money" to establishing and dissolving the charity.

Meghan and Harry announced in April 2020 that "Archewell" would be the name of their new foundation, which would replace Sussex Royal.

The name is derived from the Greek word "arche," which means "source of activity" and served as the basis for the son's name. The name Archewell was registered in the US. In October of 2020, it opened its website formally.

CHAPTER 7

How His Memoir Could Destroy The Royal Family

Axes, swords, arrows, longbows, drowning in a vat of wine, syphilis, falling off the occasional horse, a hunting "accident," gout, hubris, and various monarchs' unquenchable desire to invade France have all brought down English kings throughout the long, winding history of their millennia-plus reign.

Could King Charles III, however, be the first king to fall victim to a Macbook Air? (Death by 1,000 characters?)

When precisely Prince Harry, Duke of Sussex's book will reach the shelves and what the devil he is getting ready to tell about his titled family are now two of the publishing industry's most tightly kept secrets.

The question that courtiers, anybody with an HRH, and even the most junior footmen must undoubtedly want addressed is: How much harm would this literary IED cause to the rookie monarch and Queen Camilla? Imagine a hand grenade being thrown directly into the Buckingham Palace courtyard.

Let's hope Charles didn't get a chance to browse The Daily Beast on Monday with his cup of Earl Grey and shortbread finger for lunch if he had been seeking any form of comfort.

The news on the book front is bad for Charles, according to the Beast's impeccable-sourced royal writer Tom Sykes. One royal insider said that one chapter in particular "may mean major disaster" for the 72-year-old. (Perhaps Charles might consider attempting to retake Normandy as a diversion?)

Is it any wonder, therefore, that Sykes claims there is "increasing concern in the royal family's inner circle over the substance of Prince Harry's memoir"?

What's particularly intriguing is that, according to reports, neither Harry and wife Meghan, Duchess of Sussex's mysterious Netflix documentary nor the new season of The Crown, with its lavish recreation of Charles' philandering, tampon-fancying ways, are causing Palace brows to furrow and fountain pens to be bit.

Oh no. Sykes claims that the "courtiers are moderately sanguine" about these initiatives.

The duchess, after all, has succeeded in making herself appear boring and ridiculous in two high-profile interviews over the past two months. Meghan is just as fascinating and perceptive without her marriage and her well-known in-laws as you might anticipate a B-list actress from a mediocre cable comedy to be. In other words, she has a pathological inability to avoid talking about herself. Speaking of being lifted by your own PR

But who is her spouse? For royal aides, "Harry's book is perceived as a distinct order of danger" since he is a whole different kettle of fish.

The duke's life, personality, and career were all shaped by his royal rank for 35 years. When Diana, Princess of Wales, decided to spill the beans to Andrew Morton, she had only been married to the Windsor family for 10 years, with all the associated grief and agony that appears to be part and parcel of that job.

The duke, however, is able to draw on a lifetime's worth of discoveries, gossip, and secrets, in addition to the Viking-sized combat axe he has with his family. That confluence of exceptional insider information, such as how Princess Anne creates her famous backcombed pouf, and decades' worth of complaints?

It's possible that this book may wind up becoming the Gunpowder Plot 2.0.

Harry's attitude does not seem to have changed despite the passing of his grandmother, according to the Beast, which claims that "the potential of Harry mounting a full-blooded attack on the monarchy" is causing "anxiety" among royal insiders.

Valentine Low, the royal editor of The Times and the author of the shocking new book Courtiers: The Hidden Power Behind The Crown, reportedly informed Sykes that he was aware of a meeting that Harry had while in London with a private person (not a member of the Palace staff). Harry was gently advised to be lenient with his family in the novel.

How well did the advice go over? It sounds like it would be comparable to a vegan scotch egg at a shooting lunch. According to Low, Harry "was not very receptive to the idea."

The fact that J.R. Moehringer, a Pulitzer Prize winner, is serving as the ghostwriter for the Duke of Sussex's book, will further distinguish it. Earlier this year, renowned royal biographer Robert Lacey revealed to the Guardian that Harry had "intense interviews" with Moehringer just before the Queen's Platinum Jubilee while he was "at just about peak rage."

Page Six was informed in July by a publishing source that the book is "juicy," and a second source added that "there is some information in there that should make his family worried."

The timing is what really gets Charles in trouble here.

Only a few months into his reign, the monarch simply lacks the popular support necessary to successfully fend off a full-frontal assault by his own son, if that is what the book ultimately becomes.

Only lately has the public been prepared to overlook how Charles served as the model for lousy spouses and unimpressive fathers worldwide for decades.

(In 1991, when Prince William had hospitalization and surgery for a skull fracture after being struck in the head with a golf club at school, he demonstrated that he would never get one of those "Best Father Eva" mugs. Diana came running and spent the night at his bedside. And his father? Why, Charles scuttled off to entertain a few ministers of the government at a performance of Tosca.)

It will be a significant setback for the new Carolean age if Harry's book launches a new round of venomous charges, such as those of bad parenting, general negligence, or mistreatment by his father and/or the Palace apparatus.

Yes, His Majesty will weather the storm, but time is again a factor.

The king must be aware that, in contrast to his mother, who had 70 long years to leave her imprint, he will only hold the position of monarch for around 20 years, giving him a very limited time to make his mark on the UK and secure his opportunity to govern.

The 72-year-old can't afford to lose valuable months or years fighting PR battles or trying to discredit another relative who is busy telling the world what a terrible person he is.

There is still another option to take into account.

The Diana Chronicles and The Palace Papers author Tina Brown recently raised the possibility that the book wouldn't ever be published.

She said in an appearance at a UK literary festival earlier this month that "[The Sussexes] are now in this bind, where they've taken all this money and Harry has made this book deal where he's supposed to spill everything about his horrible life as a royal, but now he's actually tortured about it because he understands there is no way back if he does it."

I've always believed that at some point, a deal would be reached requiring Charles to repay the advance in order to prevent Harry from finishing this book.

Which would be a win-win situation. The Sussexes would receive the funds required to support their independent new lifestyle, Charles would experience a fresh wave of negative publicity, and he could spend his days bragging about his environmentally friendly Aston Martin rather than the fact that he never read his children Goodnight Moon or participated in school sporting events.

But is it possible that this Hail Mary maneuver will succeed? Harry is responsible for pulling off the publishing coup of the millennium for Penguin Random House, and if this book does "spell big trouble" for the newly crowned king, it may become a record-breaking all-time bestseller.

At the end of the day, I can only state one thing with certainty: What is it like to be king? It's a game for thugs. Your family will kill you if the French or the arrows do not.

Printed in Great Britain
by Amazon